Thoughts and Mysteries

Acrostic Poetry

Jessica Phibbs

STA BOOKS

Published by STA BOOKS 2018
www.spencerthomasassociates.com

Copyright © Jessica Phibbs 2018
ISBN. 978-0-9933957-4-1

The right of Jessica Phibbs to be identified as The Author of this work has been asserted by her in accordance with the Copyright, Designs and Patents Act 1988.

No part of this publication may be reproduced, stored in or introduced into a retrieval system, or transmitted in any form, or by any means (electronic, mechanical, photocopying, recording or otherwise) without the prior written permission of the publisher. Any person who does any unauthorised act in relation to this publication may be liable to criminal prosecution and civil claims for damages.

ACKNOWLEDGEMENT

After my mother died, I met the remarkable and wonderful Fiona Spencer Thomas, who believed in me enough to encourage and help me create this book, without whom it never would have happened, and to whom I am eternally grateful. I would also like to thank Mary Laing for her invaluable kindness and support and Charles Carey for his much-needed help and tolerance. Without them I would have given up years ago. Finally, I would like to thank my IT tutor, Janice Cheatley, without whom it would have all been impossible.

For Mother

INTRODUCTION

Many thoughts and mysteries pass through my mind, as I endeavour to introduce my first book of poems – the first book I have ever written. You may wonder how and why I first started writing acrostic poetry, also when and why I left it so late. Well, I am really not a poet at all, but a musician, who no longer plays, (though once a musician, always a musician). I started the violin aged three, the piano at eight, and also studied the viola at the London College of Music where I gained diplomas in all three instruments in the mid-1980s. I went on to teach violin and piano briefly, and continued my studies for some years. I also played chamber music, as well as in many different orchestras.

Having lived, with my family in Pimlico, London, from the age of four, (I was born in Uplyme, on the Devon/Dorset border), in 1991 I moved to Mile End in the East End of London, remaining there until 2009. I returned to Pimlico, moving into the flat where I now live to be near to my mother whose health was failing. She remained in the old family home. I had to give up my music when I moved to the flat, as my neighbours wouldn't have put up with the noise, and there certainly wouldn't have been enough room for the grand piano. I gave my violin to my Godmother and my viola had been stolen some years earlier.

I cared for my mother, Antoinette Kirkwood, until she died in January 2014. She was an exceptionally talented composer who certainly should be better known, and arranged a concert of her music which was performed in July 2017, and was a stunning success. While I was looking after her, in May 2012, I was talking on the phone to my niece, Georgina, then aged 10, when she mentioned that she'd been learning to write acrostic poetry at school. I had no idea what the word 'acrostic' meant, then my brother called to Georgina to end the conversation before I could ask her about it. I asked my mother who was in bed next to me, but she had no idea either. I went home that evening, looked the word up in my dictionary, and, discovering that a single acrostic poem (double or triple were beyond me!) was one where the initial letters of each line spelled a word or words, the following morning I wrote my first acrostic poem.

Jessica (for Mother)

Just as in the midst of time
Everyone thinks of a certain rhyme
So one lays one down to rest
Sure to sleep and dream if blest
If only night though dark is safe
Care will disappear, and chafe
Angry and hateful, only at moonbeams.
31st May 2012

I never would have written another if it hadn't been for Gwyneth George, the cellist, sadly no longer with us and a great friend of mine, very much alive at the time, who loved 'Jessica' and demanded a 'Gwyneth' poem.

Gwyneth

Great things will come to the world one day
When time slips by, the wise will say
'Yet a while, wait a while, be calm, be at peace
Never rush, worry not, life has too short a lease,
Even youth disappears, love comes and goes,
Trouble also fluctuates, as all the world knows,
Hope fills your heart, grace comes at last'.
23rd July 2012

I have continued to write acrostic poems ever since, as often as I could whilst caring for my mother, and subsequently seldom missing a day.

To end this introduction, here is a poem I wrote in 2013, which says all that needs to be said.

Introduction

I'm Jessica, I try to write
New words of comfort and delight
To pacify the troubled mind
Restoring beauty, pure and kind
Offering hope to all concerned
Delivering wisdom I have learned
Utilizing inner power
Celebrating every hour
Telling all I've come to know
Inspired, with help and strength to show
Other mortals loving ways,
Nocturnal rest and graceful days.
25 April 2013

Thoughts and Mysteries

Antoinette

Another world, another time
No-one hears me at all
To speak, and try to mime
Or be dumb, and try to call
If I see truth, then I am strong
Never hiding from the light
Ever brave, I still belong
To life itself, however slight.
Turning back, I see night fade
Enchantment comes, the price is paid.
August 22nd 2012

Archibald

An African Grey of great renown
Resplendent and noble, yet eager to please
Cheerful and kindly, he never feels down
Happy to live life in plenty and ease
Impeccable manners show class at its height
Beauty and grace show in all of his ways
Attractive and spruce, a bird of delight
Loving and caring, serenely he stays
Day-dreaming marvellous Archibald thoughts.
16th June 2013

Autumn Rain

Accepting nature's slow decay
Under raindrops as they fall
Telling tales of love's dismay
Unburdening the souls of all
Mortals this nostalgic season
Needing comfort, knowing reason…

Reborn as droplets still descend
As one forgives and shall forget
Imperfect hearts which soon shall mend
Now autumn rain shows no regret.
13th September 2013

Another Poem

Another poem, yet to write,
Now fills my mind, I contemplate
Our world, as day drifts into night,
Thoughts of beauty, love and hate,
Hell and heaven, still abound,
Every feeling, sight and sound
Reflects or echoes; all around –

Precious words are mine to give,
Offered through unending time,
Each one may disappear, or live,
Miraculously, in this rhyme.
12th December 2015

Without My Poetry

Without my poetry, I seem
Incapacitated, dead,
Though life continues, as my dream
Harmonizes all I've read,
Or heard, or seen, to make this rhyme
Unusually lovely; time
Tells my story, as I climb –

Mountains, or just into bed –
Yes, I must rest my weary head –

Perhaps I should explain, I've been
Overnight in hospital,
Enchanted to be home, I've seen
The world of medicine thrive in all
Reality, in front of me,
Yet lost without my poetry.
1st June 2017

Fast Asleep

Fast asleep, alone, I rest
And dream of joys I now forget;
Simple nature knows the best
Time for everything, and yet –

As life goes on around me, I
Slumber deeply, unaware,
Like one whose soul need never die
Eternally, whose hope is there,
Ever-present, so I'll keep
Pleasant thoughts, whilst fast asleep.
2nd June 2017

Graceful Days

Gone is sorrow, all my grief,
Regret and bitterness is past,
As graceful days bring sweet relief,
Circumstances change, at last
Enmity is over, dying,
Freeing me to live again
Unfettered, liberated, trying,
Learning to be loved, and then –

Dreaming through these precious hours,
Another season passes by,
Your world, as mine, is new, time flowers,
Softly, silently, but why?
3rd June 2017

Priorities

Profoundly, beautifully aware,
Reaching for the fragile truth,
I live and breathe this earthly air,
Only to reveal my youth
Returning, in its loveliness,
Imperfect though my life has been,
Though time may never wait to bless
Immaturity, I've seen
Enough to know that I must seize
Such gifts – my own priorities.
4th June 2017

Ornamentally (for Antoinette)

Ornamentally, her grace
Reflected beauty's subtle power,
Night's magnitude, dawn's love, her face
An image of her mind; each hour
My mother lived, her loveliness
Expressed her wisdom, strength and truth,
No longer of this world, I bless
The memory, her age, her youth;
Alive eternally, her dreams
Light my way, to lead me where
Lost time awaits, her presence seems
Yet with me, as the morning air.
5th June 2017

When All Is Gone

When all is gone, perhaps I'll learn
How beauty vanishes away
Entirely, yet my dreams shall turn
Night's darkness into glory's day –

As I may still find strength to be
Like one whose mind lives wild and free,
Like one whose eyes shall wake to see –

Illusions of some sweet tomorrow,
Stranger than this worldly sorrow –

Given hope, it seems that I
Obscure the truth, which rests upon
Nothing but the reason why
Earth still revolves, when all is gone.
6th June 2017

Finally There

Finally there, I have my own
Imagination free at last,
No longer troubled, still, alone,
At peace, I write of moments past,
Life happening and yet to be,
Lost love and immortality,
Your dreams and mine, our history –

The hours which never seem to wait,
Happiness, I contemplate
Earth's beauty, living everywhere,
Remembered days, with words to share
Each thought – perhaps I'm finally there.
7th June 2017

Solitary Mind

So shall this solitary mind
Overcome its sense of grief?
Learn of loveliness, to find
Imagination's fond relief?
The world within my loneliness
Assumes the aspect of desire,
Revealing beauty's needfulness,
Yearning hope – a burning fire –

Making me as one who feels
Inspiration in her heart,
Not knowing if its life conceals
Depths of truth, or love of art.
8th June 2017

Unpredictably

Unpredictably, life seems
New each precious, passing day,
Possibilities and dreams
Return as truths, the games we play
End up as actualities,
Daring me, at times, to write,
Insisting on such words as these,
Causing me to wonder – right
Takes the place of every wrong,
As all that lives must surely die,
But every evil must belong,
Like life, to earth itself, as I
Yield, so unpredictably.
9th June 2017

Whilst Writing

Whilst writing this, I think of how
Happiness seems far away,
In some imagined world, as now
Life beckons me, the gentle day
Speaks beautifully of hours past,
Time vanishes, returns; at last –

Without a friend to comfort me,
Relieve my sorrow, soothe my mind,
I sense hope's subtle mystery,
Thoughts of joy enchant, I find
Inspiration waiting there,
Now, as glory fills the air,
Grace turns to love, alive, aware.
10th June 2017

Tentatively

Tentatively, as I try
Each word that hovers in my mind,
Now that I awake, and my
Time to write arrives, I find
A world of possibilities,
The universe of thought is mine,
Images, ideas like these
Very humble lines, define
Exactly how the moment feels,
Like all that lives, its truth reveals
Your love and mine, so tentatively.
11th June 2017

Promised Words

Promised words, their beauty falling,
Raining, from the summer skies,
Or beckoning, commanding, calling
Me from heaven – all that dies,
In sin, may yet be raised in glory,
So goes our tale, as yet untold,
Earth's own, the truth, a living story,
Dreamt of in our hearts: the old –

World of our captivity,
Our vice and our iniquity,
Regret and sorrow, disappears,
Dissolves, as sunlight dries our tears,
Shines through love's everlasting years.
12th June 2017

Precious Time

Perhaps these hours shall wait for me,
Returning, as sweet, precious time
Echoes through the century,
Cascading through the years, as I'm
Immortal in imagination,
Obscure, and yet I'll never die
Unendingly, the explanation
Shows within these lines, as I –

Tell my tale, so beautifully,
Inconceivably, it seems,
My world remains, so mercifully
Eternal, in my living dreams.
13th June 2017

Always There

Always there, my poetry
Lingers in the living mind,
Whilst my frail mortality,
Alive within these lines, may find
Yesterday returns again,
Shadows of my world remain –

Time past survives in memories,
Harmonies and discords sound,
Echoing strange melodies,
Reverberating thoughts surround
Earth's endlessness, and words like these.
14th June 2017

Unquestioning

Unquestioning simplicity
Now fills my ordinary mind,
Quietness, felicity,
Unknown to those who ask; I find
Each word forms slowly, as I write,
Seemingly inevitably,
Time, forever out of sight,
Illusive and interminably
Of a beauty of its own,
Necessitates mortality,
I sense what I have always known,
Not losing my morality,
Guided, and unquestioning.
15th June 2017

Travelling

Travelling within my mind,
Reaching for such far-off lands
As leave all bitterness behind,
Vast oceans, moon-lit beaches, sands
Endless in their loveliness,
Lost in half-remembered dreams,
Living in their emptiness,
Imagined truth, their beauty seems
Naturally pure, to bring
Gentle thoughts, whilst travelling.
16th June 2017

Uneventfully

Uneventfully, the day,
Now over, reached its quiet end,
Each moment passed unnoticed, pray
Value it, its powers send
Eternal messages of truth,
Naturally beautiful,
Time vanishes, age conquers youth,
Finite life is wonderful,
Uncertain, always incomplete,
Lost hours, uncared for, still exist,
Like love itself, forever sweet,
Yet lovely, as the glory missed.
17th June 2017

Immeasurably

I wake to live another day,
Made lovely in its strange perfection,
Mine alone, in some, sweet way,
Earth's own, in gentle recollection,
As so many gone before,
So many more, perhaps, to be
Unveiled to such that wonder, or
Remain unmoved, immeasurably
Attracted to such thoughts, my mind
Betrays its innocent delight,
Lost in dreams love left behind –
Youth ages, morning turns to night.
18th June 2017

Quiet Wisdom

Quiet wisdom sometimes finds
Unearthly grace in mortal minds,
Intelligence and loveliness,
Enlightenment, a blessedness
Transcending all in gentleness –

Whilst writing this, my soft, sweet eyes
Imagine thoughts, and worlds, that seem,
Surely, only for the wise,
Dependent on a living dream
Of heavenly delight and power
Made free for all to find, this hour.
19th June 2017

Compulsory

Compulsory words slip through my mind,
Onto the awaiting page,
Moving fingers write, I find
Patience lingers, passion's rage,
Unknown to my sweet-tempered heart,
Lurks within another's soul,
So my love, my work, my art,
Overwhelms, with fond control,
Remaining, as my thoughts come faster
Yet, to please their living master.
20th June 2017

Insecurity

Insecurity comes creeping
Nearer, as the day begins,
Summer clouds of rain are weeping
Earthly tears for all our sins,
Christening the world with sorrow,
Understanding, pure relief,
Remorse which springs from love; tomorrow
I may find the lost belief
That harmony is of the mind,
Your thoughts a mirror to the blind.
21st June 2017

Quite Content

Quite content with what I've got,
Unused to others' company,
I sit here writing, well or not,
Time passes, all the world I see
Enchants my loving eyes…

Could it be I'll never know
Of hatred's ugly cruelty?
Never know of grief, or grow
Tired of life? So heavenly
Each treasured, earthly moment seems,
Now waking to continued dreams,
To find I'm quite content.
22nd June 2017

Little Girl

Like one forever young inside,
I'm just a little girl, at heart,
Time never changes me, I've tried
To grow within my world, my art,
Learning only how to stay,
Eternally, myself – I may –

Gradually fade and die,
In years to come, yet still be there,
Remaining in my words, as I
Leave the child to earthly care.
23rd June 2017

Thirst For Life

The hour awaits within my heart,
However strange this thirst for life
Inside me seems to be, I start
Reacting to my world – its strife
Seems endless – hatred, love and laughter
Timelessly returning – after –

Foraging for words, as my
Older days come nearer, I
Realize that I shall die –

Leaving fragments of a dream,
Illusions of what might have been
Forgotten, passing thoughts that seem
Expectant, beauty yet unseen.
24th June 2017

Much Too Tired

Much too tired, just now, to write,
Uncertainly, I try to start
Creating poetry, I might
Happen on success – my art –

Takes over, as it seems that I
Overcome exhaustion, my
Other self triumphant – why –

The hell did I get up today?
I ponder on this mystery,
Regretting nothing, anyway,
Even as your honesty
Describes this as a travesty.
25th June 2017

My Monday Waits

My Monday waits for me today,
Yesterday so far away –

Mere hours linger in my mind,
Our lives just seem to disappear,
Night follows day, and yet I find
Dreams make reality seem near,
As all who know of love and sorrow,
Yours and mine, may see tomorrow –

Welcoming another dawn,
Another moment, lost in time,
I seize my chances, was I born
To work and play with words that rhyme?
Still my Monday waits.
26th June 2017

Compliments (for Mary Laing)

Causing me such pleasure, you
Offer precious words of praise,
Meaningfully lovely, due,
Perhaps, to one who spends her days
Learning from each earthly hour,
Illuminating all she sees
Mentally, her mortal power
Engaged in composition – these
Naturally, take time to write,
Thought and skill – your kindness might
Send compliments, to my delight.
27th June 2017

My Poor Child

My poor child, what shall be your end?
Your soul is mine, my heart your friend –

Proving we are one, alone,
Of a strength and grace concealed
Or hidden from this world, we've known
Reality, the truth revealed –

Choosing actuality,
Honesty, with eyes to see
Impressions of the world to be:
Like stars that fade from heaven, given
Dawn's delight, for which we've striven.
28th June 2017

Growing Old

Gently dreaming of the past,
Realizing all that lives
On earth must come to die, at last,
Whilst hope and love, and all that gives
Illumination to the mind
Need never disappear – I find
God's grace in everything, inclined –

Or grateful to believe what's told,
Left wondering, my thoughts unfold,
Dreaming gently, growing old.
29th June 2017

Unread Rhymes (On a 1920 edition of poems by Alfred Noyes with uncut pages)

Unread rhymes of loveliness,
New-seen by my unworthy eyes,
Revealed in their deliciousness,
Excellence of thought, which lies,
As poetry, on pages I
Divided, cut – the reason why –

Radiant words, like these, remained
Hidden for so many years,
Years when others might have gained
Much joy from their delights, appears
Enigmatic to my mind –
Such beauty waits for all to find.
30th June 2017

Before I Start

Before I start to write my rhymes,
Even as my thoughts begin
Forming words, these living times,
Of beauty, horror, grace and sin,
Reveal their ever-changing ways,
Everlasting moments – days –

Imagined soon becoming real –

Soon this world of tragedy
Turns to one of joy, I feel
A strangeness in my soul, I see
Reflections in my mind, my heart
Takes precedence, before I start.
1st July 2017

Perhaps Tomorrow

Playing with my solitude,
Every gentle shadow seems
Reflective of love's gratitude,
Harmonizing all my dreams,
Appealing to my softened eyes,
Perhaps tomorrow, all that dies
Shall live, in paradise…

Telling tales of ages past,
Our stories speak of days to be,
Mine and yours, our thoughts shall last,
Overpowering time, to see
Regret and sorrow disappear,
Revealing truth and loveliness,
Our world of darkness, death and fear,
Wake to one of blessedness.
2nd July 2017

My Disarray

Muddled by the morning light,
Young as freedom, old as night –

Determined, in my disarray,
Irrational, I wake and rise,
Surrounded by the living day,
A world of doubt within my eyes;
Reaching through my ageing mind,
Resembling beauty's certainty
And truth, is love – these words shall find
Years tumbling through eternity.
3rd July 2017

Too Much Fun (for A&E)

Too much fun for me, a child
Of fifty-three, the night was wild,
Or so it seemed, to one whose mild –

Mortality is normally
Untainted by bright lights and laughter,
Colourful hilarity
Happens rarely, so that after –

Feasting happily, could one
Unleashed, a new year just begun,
Now write of having too much fun?
4th July 2017

Hidden From Me

Hidden from me, silently
Invisible, the day ahead,
Devoid of substance formerly,
Develops – all that's done or said
Evaporates into the past,
Night beckons me – shall beauty last?

Friendship? Or the world we knew?
Reality is sometimes strange
Or ugly, seen by very few
Mortal eyes, its depths of change –

Miraculous, divine, its glory
Evanescent, hidden from me.
5th July 2017

Unreadiness

Unready, these sweet, mortal eyes,
New to these immortal days,
Remain unseeing, strangely wise,
Enlightened, in their blinded ways,
As unprepared, uncertain, knowing
Death is ever-present, they
Illuminate my thoughts, and showing
Natural delight, they may
Enchant my dreams with blessedness,
Soft symphonies of loveliness,
Still lost in their unreadiness.
6th July 2017

Your Every Day (for Antoinette Kirkwood)

Your every day was beautiful,
Obscurely lovely in my mind,
Unsullied, as the bountiful
Reflections of your love shall find –

Expression in your thoughts, tonight,
Veiled in mystery, your dreams,
Eternal as the morning light,
Return as music, sound that seems
Your very soul at play…

Depicting all you used to say,
As one whose life was never grey,
Your world, your art, your every day.
7th July 2017

Mere Poetry (for Antoinette Kirkwood)

Morning comes, and how can I
Express in words the perfect grace,
Resurgent joy and thanks that my
Elation shows? Your living face –

Personality and power
Of thought remain within my mind,
Expressed within your music; our
Talents differ, as I find,
Reacting to the worlds we see,
Your worth out-weighs mere poetry.
8th July 2017

Dimmed Sight

Death beckons, gently, lovingly,
It seems my sight is dimmed by truth,
Made obscure; caressingly,
Merging with the light, my youth
Entices me from far away,
Delighting in sweet yesterday –

Sweet moments in my softened past,
Impressions lost within my mind
Gradually form, at last
Hope promises, however blind,
To brush away my tears.
9th July 2017

Month Of Mine

Month of mine, this sweet July
Of sunshine, when my soul was born,
Naturally free, and I
Transformed my world, one summer morn,
Heaven-blest with love…

Often life was troubled, strange,
Fearful, sometimes lovely, change –

Made my richly-coloured years
Improbable; my thoughts incline,
Now as this season passes, nears
Extinction, to this month of mine.
10th July 2017

To Please You

To please you, coax and satisfy,
Or soothe your very soul, I try –

Picturesque words, such as these
Luminous delights, which seem
Enough to set your heart at ease,
And leave your mind at peace, to dream
Sweet dreams of living loveliness,
Even as their joys caress –

Your innermost desires, and slip through
Other-worldly thoughts – a fool's few
Unimportant lines, to please you.
11th July 2017

Slight Regret

So shall my talent slip away,
Like a shadow of the night,
Invisible at break of day,
Gone forever? Thoughts that might
Hover in my wakeful mind,
Troubled images, the kind –

Reasoning cannot dispel,
Envelop me; I cannot sleep,
Gently dreaming all is well,
Reaching through my world, the deep
Eternity of life, to let
Tomorrow bring a slight regret.
12th July 2017

For The Moment

For the moment, passing by,
Or vanishing so quickly, I
Recount my feelings, I may die –

Tomorrow, live a thousand years,
Happily to write, my fears
Evaporate, through smiles and tears –

Made lovely in imagination
Only, lasting beautifully,
Moonlit hours of contemplation,
Ever-present, wonderfully
Nearing sweet eternity,
The world surrounding you and me.
13th July 2017

False Dreams

False dreams, which turn my world around,
And tell me lies I would believe,
Lies which make each sight and sound
Seem real – such strange ideas achieve
Enactment of desire…

Demonstrating how I feel
Respecting love and life and death,
Expressing thoughts I would conceal,
As every heartbeat, every breath,
Mingles with a mind that seems
Suppressed – the truth survives false dreams.
14th July 2017

Endeavouring

Endeavouring, through passing years,
Never-endingly, to write,
Demonstrating love, which clears
Earth's mystery, reflecting light,
A world of thought, and hope, and dreams,
Virtue, truth and loveliness
Of heart, a universe that seems
Untainted by the wretchedness
Remaining in humanity,
I reach through mortal doubt, to find
Nature's strength, as vanity
Gives way to beauty's peace of mind.
15th July 2017

Cornucopias

Created out of silver, to
Overflow with sweet delights,
Replete with goodness, all that you
Need ever wish for – golden nights,
Unbroken, lead to precious days,
Cornucopias of love,
Of joys and beauties to amaze,
Perplex the senses, from above,
Impressions of Utopia
Abound, my cornucopia
Seems like a paradise.
16th July 2017

Brighter Hours (on a religious text)

Brighter hours of love are mine,
Reflected in each precious letter,
Illumined in each word divine,
Greeting me, to make me better;
Having special properties,
Taking me where heavens are
Eternal, free, and wake to seize
Reality, as, near or far –

Happiness shall come to me,
Oppression, fear and doubt shall end,
Uncertainty and misery
Recede, and God shall be my friend,
Surrounding brighter hours.
17th July 2017

Transforming

Transforming lives with poetry,
Removing obstacles of hate,
Attracting truth and certainty,
New worlds of loveliness await;
Suddenly, within your mind,
Freedom calls, a gentle voice
Of love, your eyes, no longer blind,
Reveal a universe of choice,
Made, seemingly, for you alone,
Illuminated by your heart,
Now, as the life you've always known,
Gradually falls apart.
18th July 2017

Living It Up

Life proceeds inevitably,
Inexplicably the same,
Virtue seems so perfectly
Inviolable, my days are tame,
Never knowing freedom's fun,
Golden spirit – am I one –

Imagination left behind
To wander purposeless and blind –

Untouched by worlds of light and glory?
Perhaps tonight's a different story.
19th July 2017

Strange Nights

Strange nights, which lead to living days,
Times of loveliness and sorrow,
Reaching through unfathomed ways,
Arriving at some sweet tomorrow,
Now waiting in my beating heart,
Greeting me, as I shall start
Each morning knowing dawn must part –

New moments from the hours before,
In darkness, dreams of preparation
Gently fill my mind with more
Harmony and exultation
Than paradise can hold – delights
Soft shadows leave on such strange nights.
20th July 2017

Forever Friday

Forever Friday, in my mind,
Oppressed by love, this quiet day
Reaches through my heart, to find
Endless beauty – clouds of grey
Veil the perfect summer skies;
Even as my gentle eyes
React, the moment lives and dies –

Forever Friday, in my soul,
Remembering these hours of sorrow,
Infiltrating lives, the whole
Day seems just as if tomorrow
Always waits, to come again,
Yet Friday ever shall remain.
21st July 2017

Already Written

As almost all has been before,
Little can be said that's new,
Reality seems even more
Elusive than the words that you
Are reading at this moment, I
Dream and wake and live to die,
Yet know not of the reason why –

We speak of precious hours past,
Recent times and days to be,
I know the future may outlast
These lines, they may not live to see
The dawn, I taste the apple bitten,
Eve's and Adam's hearts were smitten,
No thoughts but those already written.
22nd July 2017

Soft Silence

Soft silence speaks to me so well,
Of hope, desire and loveliness,
Freedom, strength, its powers tell
The truth in all its endlessness –

Simplicity of thought, its strange
Immediacy, my waking mind
Listens quietly, as change
Eclipses all that's left behind,
Naturally, forever new,
Created for the void that you
Encounter in these words.
23rd July 2017

My Patience

Made, in solitude, to wait,
Yet knowing it may be too late –

Possibly, to find success,
As talent thrives in many minds,
To flourish, mine is more or less
Invisible, its beauty finds
Elusive words of poetry,
New-formed, for my delight alone,
Created gently, patiently,
Expressed in truths as yet unknown.
24th July 2017

Difficulties

Difficulties, which may seem
Insurmountable, may be
Forever in our minds, a dream
For which we wish, a fantasy,
Ideal in our imaginations,
Charming us, this living hour,
Until its very complications
Light our way, with subtle power
To overcome our deepest fears,
Illuminate our world of night,
Enrich our days, fulfil our years
So sweetly, heal our blinded sight.
25th July 2017

Out Of My Mind

Overflowing beauty streams,
Unbidden, from my heart, which seems
To be a paradise of dreams –

Of perfect loveliness, which lives
From hour to hour, a world that gives –

Meaning to the passing years,
Yours and mine, tomorrow nears –

Maybe I shall live to see
Infinity, and I shall find
No end to this strange world, and be
Declared insane, out of my mind.
26th July 2017

Feeling Happy

Feeling happy, as I wake,
Enjoying life, without a reason,
Even as my senses make
Light of all my fears, the season
Illustrates a world of such
Nonsensical delights, with much
Gaiety, which seems to touch –

Humanity, and even though
Apparent joy can never last,
Perhaps these words will serve to show
Proof that love is unsurpassed,
Yet manifest within.
27th July 2017

Three Years Old

Three years old, I came to know
How agonizing death could be,
Realized how love could show
Every blessing, now I see
Exactly what was mine…

Yet even then, I was alone,
Entirely, in my childish mind,
Accepting life – I've never grown,
Remaining beautifully blind,
Seeing from within…

Only now the story's told,
Like a dream, its depths unfold
Distinctly, I was three years old.
28th July 2017

Thanks To You (for Charles)

The world is mine, I seem to be
Happy just to live as one
Attracted by its grace, to see
No ugliness; this work, begun,
Knowing gratitude of mind,
Sweeps through my soul, until I find –

The words that you deserve to hear,
Or read; your strength, forever near –

Yet always far, and slipping through
Our separation, wakes anew;
Unseen, I write, all thanks to you.
29th July 2017

Most Important

My most important work today,
Obviously, seems to be
Shining through these words, which say
Too much, yet not enough, for me –

Illustrating how my mind
Moves in ways which can't be told,
Possibly my thoughts shall find
Other worlds, in days of old,
Relics of what might have been
The ending, but were just the start,
As, everywhere, there lives, unseen,
Not realized, yet in each heart,
The answer to our dreams.
30th July 2017

Requited Love

Reappearing constantly,
Even as the feeling seems
Quenched by hopelessness, to be
Unwelcome in my heart, my dreams
Imitate reality,
Telling truths as yet unseen,
Explaining so persuasively,
Demonstrating all that's been –

Lost in my uncertain mind,
Overcome by thoughts above
Verity itself, to find
Enlightenment, requited love.
31st July 2017

Pleasing Me

Puzzling over what to write,
Like one who's hard to satisfy
Entirely, seemingly, I might
Acquire a taste for truth, as I
Select the words I like the best,
Interpreting the way I feel,
Not without a certain zest,
Glad to find my thoughts reveal –

My happiness in all I see –
Earth's sacred beauty, pleasing me.
1st August 2017

Pretty Words

Pretty words – how can they seem
Remotely like good poetry?
Evolving thoughts, the human dream,
Turn truth into dishonesty,
Time into an endless void,
Your knowledge might be best employed –

Writing of the world you see
Observed within your living eyes,
Rejecting all uncertainty –
Doubt lingers – freedom's beauty dies –
Shadows form such pretty words.
2nd August 2017

Made For You

Made for you, this work of art
Allows for every thought you feel,
Dream or image of the heart,
Emotion you would fain conceal –

Favouring your inner senses,
Obscure desires, coincidences,
Reaching through your soul's defences –

Yesterday you thought you knew
Our world, yet ever slipping through,
Unseen, was heaven, made for you.
3rd August 2017

Wakeful Mind

Writing this, it seems to me
As if this gentle, lovely hour
Keeps my secret, silently,
Expectantly – its subtle power
Frees my soul; my inner being,
Unused to liberty, unseeing,
Lost in quietude…

Moments pass, and suddenly
I feel that I'm no longer blind,
No longer lost, life's mystery
Depicted in my wakeful mind.
4th August 2017

Time To Wonder

Time to wonder how on earth
I ever wrote a line before,
My gift, and all my talent's worth
Evaporate, this work seems more –

Than ever of a hopelessness,
Or uselessness, and more or less –

Written just to prove that I
Only ever write to show
Nothing but the reasons why
Dunces like me never know
Exactly what to write about –
Reasons you must do without.
5th August 2017

Kept Living

Kept living by my poetry,
Even as my thoughts survive
Perpetually, joyfully,
Time spinning through my mind, alive –

Long after my mortality
Immortalizes every word,
Verity of heart may be
Illusory, yet I have heard
None deny the loveliness
Growing through my endlessness.
6th August 2017

Enabling Me

Enabling me, my world of dreams,
Now, as ever, in my mind,
As lovely as my soul, which seems
Beautiful as dawn – the blind
Look within your gentle eyes,
Imagination's innocence,
Nature's force, which lives and dies
Grasping truth's intemperance –

My everlasting liberty,
Earth's strange delights, enabling me.
7th August 2017

Just Nobody

Just nobody, a simple fool,
Unnoticed by this earth, as I
Studiously write, as you'll
Take time to read, and that is why –

New words fall from my moving pen,
Only for your gentle eyes –
Beautiful as morning, when
Our world appears, impartial, wise,
Discerning what no others see –
You're wonderful, I'm nobody.
8th August 2017

Unwillingly

Unwillingly, I try to write,
Now that morning comes, and I
Wrest the meaning from the night –
Imaginings, that live and die,
Like raindrops when the sun appears,
Leaving rainbows' vanished joy –
I sense the moments, feel the years,
Neglect the hours I should employ
Growing dreams of poetry,
Light shining through the words – I see
You laugh, I smile, unwillingly.
9th August 2017

Not Without Hope

Not without hope, or strength of mind,
Or depth of heart, I wake to find
The world of all my dreams combined –

Welcoming the day ahead,
I write these words of explanation,
Telling that I'm not yet dead,
However short my life's duration;
Our universe seems made of years
Unformed, the beauty of our tears
Transcends the sorrow of our fears –

Having written of how much
One moment lost in time can mean,
Perhaps I may yet write of such
Elusive thoughts that might have been.
10th August 2017

Before Rising

Before rising, as I wake,
Even as my dreams subside,
Free within my mind, I take
Our world into my heart; beside
Remnants of the night, I lie,
Exposed to morning's charm, as I

Remember how I used to feel,
Inside, at moments such as this;
Sweet visions permeate the real,
I sense the beauty others miss;
Negating the mundane, my eyes
Greet love's dawn, before I rise.
11th August 2017

Lovely Sorrow

Lovely sorrow comes to me,
Overwhelming me, and yet,
Very soon my eyes shall see
Each moment of life's sweet regret,
Like all I've loved, just slip away;
Yearning for the truth, I pray –

Silently, within my heart,
Only heaven knows my mind,
Remaining God's alone, I start
Reaching for His grace, to find
Our hope rests in our dreams, tomorrow
Waits, in worlds of lovely sorrow.
12th August 2017

Previously

Previously written rhymes,
Remind me all has gone before,
Even as these living times
Veil the world in dreams, with more
Illusions of reality,
Or thoughts, than beauty can possess,
Unseen, as love's humanity
Shall reach through our unwillingness,
Like truth, which shines harmoniously,
Yet all has been said previously.
13th August 2017

Too Many Words

Too many words – how can I choose
One from another? Win or lose
Our little game? Accept, refuse?

My chances seem to multiply,
As divers thoughts proliferate;
New worlds replace the old, as I
Yield to beauty, death and fate –

Whilst wondering what life can be,
Only for my heart to find
Reason forms reality,
Dreams tumble through my muddled mind –
Surrounded by too many words.
14th August 2017

Waking In The Night

Waking in the night, it seems
As though my world shall never end,
Knowing this, my strangest dreams
Incline my thoughts where angels send
Nature's messengers of love,
Greeting mortals; from above –

Illuminated heavens reign
Never-endingly; again –

These dark and silent hours reveal
How truth and gentleness conceal
Enchanted minds, where the unreal –

Nears sweet impossibility,
Illusive images run free,
Golden immortality
Holds sway, this living fantasy
Takes shape, whilst waking in the night.
15th August 2017

Broken Nights

Believing what my senses tell,
Regardless of what hour of day,
Or night, the time may be, as well-
Known images and dreams portray
Enchanted worlds, their loveliness
Near-perfect; but the truth is less –

Nice in its reality,
In its certainty, than dreams;
Given that humanity
Has untold troubles, all that seems
To startle, sudden sounds and sights,
Seem manifest, in broken nights.
16th August 2017

Little Violin

Loved, revered, within my dreams
I feel the magic of your time,
The strange Victorian age, which seems
The essence of your charm, this rhyme
Lets others see your sheer perfection,
Eighth-sized grace, my soul's reflection –

Verifies your gentle beauty,
Immaculately crafted art,
Only to confirm my duty –
Life-long care – my very heart
Implores the world of future days
Not to neglect my loving ways.
17th August 2017

Feminine Minds

Freedom lives within our hearts,
Even as we think and grow,
Merging with our souls, it starts
Immersing us in beauty; no
New delight or secret dream,
Illusion, doubt or fantasy,
No false pretence could ever seem
Enough to blight the mystery –

Made lovely, through our craft and skill,
Imagination, love and grace,
No power of darkness ever will
Deter us, as our gifts replace
Shadows in our feminine minds.
18th August 2017

Present Moment

Perhaps this present moment will
Remain, for future worlds to see,
Enshrined within these lines, and still
Softly lovely – made to be
Eternal – lost within your eyes,
Now and forever, gently wise,
The thought of love, which never dies –

My own, and yours, a memory
Of music, living in this rhyme,
Melodic words in harmony,
Encapsulating passing time,
Naturally, beautifully,
Truthfully and endlessly.
19th August 2017

No Thoughts

No thoughts of happiness or sorrow,
Or yesterday, or sweet tomorrow –

Truth is beautiful and rare,
Harmonious, yet seldom told,
Others laugh, yet some may care,
Underneath it all; the old
Gentleness I used to feel
Has gone, my mind is far away,
The images that seemed so real
Shadows in a world of grey.
20th August 2017

Repeatedly

Repeatedly, I write, pretending
Everything I say is new,
Perhaps the messages I'm sending
Entertain the happy few
Affected by my poetry,
Though I've said these things before,
Even so, they love to see
Delightful words again, with more
Lustre, as they seem to be
Yet lovelier, repeatedly.
21st August 2017

Chosen Words

Creating poetry which seems
Heavenly, is my ideal,
Our world of hopes, regrets and dreams,
Sweetness, bitterness, the real
Earth, in which this stranger lives,
Needs beauty, love, a strength that gives –

Whilst taking nothing in return,
Offering without demand,
Read these chosen words, and learn
Delight in everything, command,
Subjugate your soul.
22nd August 2017

Giving Poetry

Giving poetry is all
I live for, in my world of dreams,
Virtue, truth, as I recall
It, comes to me, in all that seems
Noble to my humble mind,
Guided through my art – a kind –

Perfected in the ancient past,
Only to enhance the years,
Expressed in gratitude, to last
Timelessly, its beauty nears
Reality, its mystery
Your own – the gift of poetry.
23rd August 2017

Optimistically

Optimistically writing,
Possibly, your masterpiece,
Telling gentle truths, exciting
Inspiration, love's release;
Marvelling at how your mind
Imagines every lovely line –
Soft sweet subtleties, which find
The way to happiness divine;
Improbable though it may seem,
Creativity remains
A grace, which once was just a dream,
Living in your heart – it gains
Limitless rewards, to be
Your servant, optimistically.
24th August 2017

My Stupidity

My stupidity of mind
Yields lovely poetry – I find –

Simple phrases come to me,
The world of truth is on my side,
Undoubtedly; my honesty
Persuades me that I cannot hide
Inherent ignorance, as I
Dream my gentle life away,
Instinctively, to live and die
The life of one who's proud to say:
'Yesterday was mine'.
25th August 2017

Little Missed (for Charles)

Left without you now, it seems,
Improbably, that life remains,
The world of echoes, thoughts and dreams
Thrives within a heart that gains
Lost beauty from your absent mind,
Even as I write, I find –

My talent and imagination
Illustrate the way I feel;
Sweeping through my concentration,
Shadows of my soul reveal
Emotions which I must resist –
Denying that you're little missed.
26th August 2017

Living Lovingly

Living lovingly, I feel
Imbued with heaven's loveliness,
Velvet dreams, their depths reveal
Imagination's endlessness,
Night's glory, which must lead to day,
Gently time must pass away –

Like life itself, and soon be gone,
Over, yet shall always seem
Veiled in mystery, as on
I journey, down its flowing stream,
Never ceasing to believe,
Guided by my soul, I see
Lost moments, hours for which I grieve,
Yet truly living lovingly.
27th August 2017

With Eagerness

With eagerness, I start to write
Immediately, without waiting,
Telling of a sweet delight,
Happy to be contemplating –

Everything that's beautiful,
And of another world, I see
Greatness, all that's wonderful,
Eternal, in life's mystery;
Repeating all that's gone before,
Nature lives in loveliness,
Evening turns to night, with more
Shadows of love's endlessness,
Secreting heaven's dawn.
28th August 2017

Ineffectually

Ineffectually, I
Near exasperation, as,
Eventually, starting my
Feeble offering, which has
Faults, which even I can see,
Exposed, I bravely carry on,
Creating something which shall be
Thought nothing of, when I am gone,
Unless, perhaps, my efforts might,
Actually, strive to find
Loveliness in what I write,
Lost meaning in my foolish mind –
Your world within my soul.
29th August 2017

Silent Thoughts

Shades of love, in quiet minds,
Invite such silent thoughts as these,
Lovely as the skies, the kinds
Enchanted by the dawns, that please
Night's dreamers, as the morning starts
To infiltrate their souls, their hearts –

To lead to yet another day,
Honouring earth's majesty,
Or sweet indifference, which may
Unfold in hours that seem to be
Gentle moments, lost in space,
Held, forever, in mid-air,
The heavenly and commonplace
Seem one, unchanging, unaware.
30th August 2017

Empty Hours

Enraptured by a thankfulness,
Made grateful for these empty hours,
Portrayed in words of gentleness,
Transcending time, their subtle powers
Yielding to my heart…

How strange this lovely void can be,
Open to interpretation,
Underneath its mystery,
Reflected through imagination,
Shines the love I miss.
31st August 2017

Enough Sleep

Enough sleep for my weary mind,
Night ends in perfect wakefulness,
Our world of dreams is left behind,
Unseen, as morning's blissfulness
Glories in another day;
How many more shall pass away –

Slowly, through this life of mine?
Little do my feelings know,
Even truth cannot divine
Everything this earth can show,
Perhaps it never will.
1st September 2017

Autumn Waits

Autumn waits, this gentle season,
Undeniably, must end;
The summer fades, as truth and reason,
Understanding, love, befriend
My weary heart, as if today
Never lived, to pass away –

Whilst writing under clear, blue skies,
Alight with dreams of heaven's power,
Invisible, all-seeing eyes
That rest within each endless hour
Summer sends, as autumn waits.
2nd September 2017

Soldier Boy

Sweet soldier boy, your beauty lives
Only in your shadowed past,
Lost within a world that gives
Delight and horror, thoughts which last
Indefinitely, in my mind,
Each bitter memory I find
Remains, your strength and grace combined –

Bring light into the depths of sorrow,
Overwhelming me, I borrow
Yesterday, to free tomorrow.
3rd September 2017

Come What Will

Come what will, my life shall be
Original, my very own,
Made beautiful, and I shall see
Earth's joy and freedom, left alone –

With everything within my heart,
Happiness seems ever mine,
A never-ending dream, I start
To feel as one who's blest – divine –

Words speak to my unworthy mind
In silence, and my thoughts are still
Lost within this world, I find
Love matters to me, come what will.
4th September 2017

September Days

So shall these sad, September days
Envelop me in loveliness,
Perfect truth, their quiet ways
Transcend these lines in gentleness?
Even so, their innocence
May rest in dreams which cannot last,
Beauty vanishes, I sense
Each moment disappear, the past
Repeats its mystery…

Deep within my mind, I wait,
As one whose patience never ends,
Yet as the hours pass, my fate
Seems lost in time the future sends.
5th September 2017

Virginia Woolf (1882-1941)

Very much in every word
I write, alive in many minds,
Remembered through the voice I've heard
Gently speaking – reason finds
Imagination lasts forever,
Necessitating beauty, your
Intelligence remains, shall never
Atrophy – what's gone before –

Will last throughout the centuries
Of darkness, ever bringing light,
Or truth, your presence lives, to ease
Lost souls, the power of your sight
Frees a captive world.
6th September 2017

That Time Again

To write of happiness and sorrow,
Hatred, love and beauty, just
As yesterday creates tomorrow,
Thinking through my dreams, I must –

Try to tell the truth, to live
Instinctively, as one who hears
Music in the silence, give
Enchantment to the passing years –

And listen, feel the pulse that beats,
Gently, in this living earth,
Acknowledging the dawn, that greets
Infinity, another birth –
Now comes that time again.
7th September 2017

Gloom Threatens

Gloom threatens, heaven's darkness reigns,
Love alone can conquer hate,
Obscurity of thought remains,
Oppressing me, I contemplate
My fate, my destiny…

Tell me, where does life begin
Harmonizing with the truth?
Reality delight to win
Earth's passion for an endless youth –
A world which knows not death, nor sorrow,
The depths of time, its cruel power?
Even as some strange tomorrow
Nears, perhaps this very hour
Shall prove to be my own.
8th September 2017

Glad To Wake

Glad to wake, and leave my dreams –
Lost thoughts of unreality –
And welcome in a world that seems
Determined by normality –

Though strange its varied ways can be,
Order comes from living free –

Whilst on this earth, I make my choice,
And liberty is no mistake,
Knowing that I have a voice,
Entirely mine, I'm glad to wake.
9th September 2017

Influentially

Influentially, it seems
Night still remains, as I awake,
Feelings rest within, as dreams
Live on, as some divine mistake;
Unknown to dawn's reality,
Eternity seems mine alone,
Natural uncertainty,
The world of truth, is not my own;
Imagination cannot last,
As lovely as it seems to be,
Lost in memories, the past
Leaves nothing but normality,
Yet lingers, influentially.
10th September 2017

As Yet Unknown

As yet unknown, this poem seems
Suspended in mid-air – my dreams –

Yield beauty, love and pure delight,
Enchantment, joy, of which I write,
Tenderly, as day meets night –

Unhindered by a mind that gives
No less than what my soul could ask,
Kindly, of it – duty lives
Nowhere but within; my task,
Once done and finished – fully grown –
Will prove what I've already shown –
New thoughts shall come, as yet unknown.
11th September 2017

Quickly Writing

Quickly writing anything
Uninteresting, speedily
I let the words the fates shall bring
Crowd the page in front of me;
Knowing nothing very much,
Learning little more, with such
Yearning – talking double Dutch –

Wasting precious earthly time,
Rightly feeling it to be
Invaluable – shall this rhyme
Turn beauty into travesty?
Into something happily
Nonsensical, that prettily
Goes on, to end quite suddenly?
12th September 2017

There You Are (for Harry)

To tell of how I wait for you,
Holding on, as every hour
Evaporates so slowly, few
Remain, as you shall come, your power
Enhances every word…

Your love and your intelligence,
Our bond, the beauty that I sense
Untainted, in your soul, from whence –

A world of dreams evolves, a star
Reflected in your eyes, from far
Elysium – and there you are.
13th September 2017

Unsteadily

Unsteadily, I rise, unsure,
Night deep within my dream-filled eyes,
Sleepily, it seems, the pure
Transience of beauty dies,
Eclipsed by dawn's reality,
A world of new-found loveliness,
Delighting in simplicity,
Immune to hatred's ugliness;
Love's presence is too much for me,
Yet still I rise, unsteadily.
14th September 2017

Childish Ways

Childless am I, growing old,
Hopeful, solitary days
Infiltrate my mind, untold
Love is mine, my childish ways,
Dependent on a fantasy,
Imagination's comforts, make
Summer in my soul, I see
Heaven in my heart, forsake –

Worldly bitterness, to live
A life where innocence and youth
Yield blind delights, and yearn to give
Sweet succour, some resurgent truth.
15th September 2017

Persistently

Pursuing me, persistently,
Each moment, every waking hour,
Remaining with me, constantly,
Sleeping with me, as its power
Immerses my beleaguered senses,
Simply yearning to be free,
To live again – without defences,
Enjoying no immunity,
Nor even strength, to ease the pain,
Troubled, anxious, as my mind
Longs for peace, for rest, in vain,
Yet love is always there, to find.
16th September 2017

Lovely Love

Light dwells within a warmth divine,
Outshining bitterness and doubt,
Veiled in softness – yours and mine –
Earth's freedom cannot do without
Lovely love, a dream that lives,
Young forever, all it gives –

Lasting through eternity,
Or through this world of new tomorrows
Vying to make history
Endure, through life's delights and sorrows.
17th September 2017

Interestingly

Interestingly enough,
Now I come to think of it,
Time and tides, the smooth and rough,
Emotions, feelings, passion, wit,
Rest within a world that sees
Everything the heart can tell,
Seemingly; a mind at ease
Takes my thoughts, my soul, as well,
Into a universe of dreams,
Nights of wonder, dawns of bliss,
Greeting me with joy, that seems
Like love – shall life remain like this,
Yet another day?
18th September 2017

Little Dreams

Lost within my little dreams,
Inspired to write each foolish line,
To live within a world that seems
Timeless – if the truth were mine –
Lovely as a summer's day –
Each moment of my life would stay –

Deep within my heart, and yet
Reality is often strange,
Even as I would forget
A past that I can never change
My thoughts, and everything I feel
Shall be as little dreams turned real.
19th September 2017

Easy Writing

Early in the day, I start,
As one who loves to write with ease,
Showing warmth and depth of heart,
Youth which ages, words like these –

Whilst all that's new is growing old,
Reacting to the truth, I find
It vanishes, as dreams unfold
Their loveliness within a mind
Impossible to quantify –
None could know the thoughts that I
Give life to – shall their beauty die?
20th September 2017

Recommending

Recognizing beauty's power,
Every grace that virtue brings,
Causing love to blossom, flower
Out of emptiness – some things –
Moments, hours of loveliness –
Make this world a better place,
Each time we fail, we find success
Nearer, as the life we face
Demands we give our very best,
Inspiring thoughts keep minds ascending,
None could make more manifest
God's word – the truth I'm recommending.
21st September 2017

After Resting

After resting, waking, rising,
Friends seem closer, none despising
Talents I may have, or follies,
Emotions such as love, which jollies,
Rescues, and remains –

Real, as gentle, autumn skies,
Evenings, dawns, which please my eyes
So much, this life, my very own,
To live, in depths of joy, alone,
Invulnerable, within a mind
None can steal, nor make unkind –
Greatness is what others find.
22nd September 2017

Truthfully

The truth is often hard to tell –
Reading minds, and thoughts, and dreams
Untainted by the bliss or hell
That studied blindness brings, which seems
Harmful – when a child can see,
From eyes unprejudiced and pure,
Unsullied, confident and free,
Loving, beautiful and sure,
Like one whose life was, youthfully,
Your own, which you lived truthfully.
23rd September 2017

Awake At Last

Awake at last, with grateful eyes,
Welcoming the precious day
Again, its beauty lives and dies,
Kindness rules, as angels play
Earth's game within my heart…

As dawn brings love, eternity
Triumphs, immortality –

Lights a world which never ends,
A future which is never past,
So I feel, as one who sends
These lines to you – awake at last.
24th September 2017

Wanting More (for Charles)

Whether I am right or wrong,
A poet or a simple fool,
Not worthy ever to belong
To literature's exclusive school,
I hear your words of warmth and praise,
Negating doubt – their beauty plays,
Gently, in my mind – each phrase –

Melody of thought, I write –
Obscurely lovely, great or poor –
Reaches to your soul, you might
Enquire for others, wanting more.
25th September 2017

Janice Cheatley

Just what I would like to say,
Admiring such good qualities,
Naturally your own, today
I know – you make complexities
Clear, as your intelligence
Empowers us all, your common sense –

Charm, and confidence, delight,
Harmonizing discord, we
Enjoy your gift of knowledge, might
Appear indifferent, yet see
The generosity of mind
Lavished on our gratitude,
Encouraged to succeed, we find
Yet more – a change of attitude.
26th September 2017

Better Things

Believing in the truth, I find
Earth's beauty, its eternity
Take precedence within a mind
That loves, as immortality
Evolves – our endless journey starts,
Reflected in our souls, our hearts –

The loveliness, of which I write,
Helps my fond imagination
Illuminate a world, which might
Need all my powers of concentration,
Gradually, to reveal
Something of the way I feel.
27th September 2017

Gladdened Eyes

Giving my imagination
Leeway, as the day appears,
Alive with beauty, explanation
Deepens into love, as tears
Dry gently, and my gladdened eyes
Enjoy the loveliness within,
No living image ever dies
Eternally – as truth shall win,
Dreams end mortality…

Even as I wake, I find
Yesterday creates tomorrow's
Everlasting grace, my mind
Sees hope, is blind to earthly sorrows.
28th September 2017

Listening To You

Listening to you, I write
Instinctively – as moments, years,
So many centuries – time's flight –
Takes me to your thoughts, love nears,
Enchanted by your living mind,
No words but these shall come, as I
Infiltrate your heart, to find,
Naturally, my own, as my
Gentle pulse beats on…

The minutes, hours, endlessness,
Obscure this world – its loveliness –

Yearning to be known as true –
Only death can be our due,
Unless I'm listening to you.
29th September 2017

Abandoned Days

Abandoned days, and vanished hours,
Beautiful, forgotten nights,
Appear within our minds, like flowers
Nurtured by a sun, which lights
Depths of fantasy, that's seen
Only in imaginations,
Neglecting all that might have been
Enough to make our concentrations
Dream of life to come…

Delighting in a world that was
Alive within a past that plays
Your games and mine, and all because
Sweet love ruled those abandoned days.
30th September 2017

Maternal Love (for Mother)

Music rules a heart that lives
As one whose passion cannot die,
That I know, and yet she gives
Eternal love to me, as I
Remain her daughter, evermore,
Nurtured by her loveliness,
A gift from one who's gone before,
Leaving me her endlessness –

Like one whose beauty is the truth,
Only known to those who see
Verity in ageless youth,
Earth's everlasting mystery.
1st October 2017

Hidden Passions

Hidden passions, secret dreams,
Illusions of a fond delight,
Depths of feeling, hope that seems
Denied to none, just out of sight –
Early dawn's sweet, sacred start,
Night's ending, worlds that fall apart –

Proving love is everything,
A concept perfectly divine,
Shining through our souls, to bring
Springtime's purity, refine
Imagination's loveliness,
Or beauty's ever-changing fashions,
None doubting heavenly success
Sublimates our hidden passions.
2nd October 2017

In Awe Of You (for Robert Sharpe)

In awe of you, with joy, I write,
Not knowing such a sweet delight –

As this, I speak about your mind –
Wonderfully knowing, kind,
Enlightened by your love, I find –

Our world within your happiness,
Friendship in your gentleness –

Your thoughts are wise, yet ever new,
Of a beauty, pure and true,
Unique, and I'm in awe of you.
3rd October 2017

Just Glimpsed

Just glimpsed, a moment, flying past,
Unknown, and partially unseen;
Shadows in my mind; at last
The time has come – what might have been –

Given, has been taken, gone,
Lost in my imagination,
I smile within, the world moves on,
My words require an explanation –
Perhaps the truth shall not be known,
Shall disappear, a tale untold,
Everything this life has shown
Depicts a moment, growing old.
4th October 2017

Immersed In Love

Immersed in love, a truth that seems
Manifest in everything
My heart encounters – living dreams –
Eternal as the skies, which bring
Rain and sunshine, day and night,
Shades of twilight – sweep my mind,
Emerging from a world that might
Deny me nothing, as I find –

Illusion in reality,
Natural disparity –

Lost, within a soul, that gains,
Or wins, that precious gift, above
Virtue's beauty, and remains,
Endlessly, immersed in love.
5th October 2017

Promised Gift

Promised gift, the coming hour,
Reason still awaits God's will,
Or judgement, as my thoughts devour
Moments yet to be, and fill
Illuminated days with joy,
So time passes happily
Enough, my heart and soul employ
Discernment, and my eyes shall see –

Gladly, what the future holds,
If all is well, and fortune kind,
Friendly, as my life unfolds
To offer what is yet to find.
6th October 2017

Unrecorded

Unrecorded time which passes,
Never shall it quite remain
Reality – through looking-glasses,
Every hour comes back again,
Comes back to haunt the troubled mind,
Or maybe just to disappear,
Reason comforts, love is kind,
Dutiful, and ever near –
Every doubt my dreams afforded
Dies in moments unrecorded.
7th October 2017

Better Poetry

Better poetry should be
Enthralling, comic, beautiful,
Timeless, sadly, happily
Transforming minds, the wonderful
Exuding from the inspiration
Reaching your imagination –

Proving greatness is not dead,
Or lost in life's obscurity,
Eternally – it must be said
That only truth's reality,
Reason, hope, morality,
Your thoughts, make better poetry.
8th October 2017

Making History

My world and yours are not the same,
As all minds differ from each other,
Knowing not from whence you came,
I feel you are a sister, brother,
Near me, even as I write,
Guiding me, as wisdom might –

Helping me to live as one
Incapable of enmity,
Sweet-tempered; I have just begun
To sense the possibility
Of living with an open heart,
Remaining with you, as you start
Your journey – making history.
9th October 2017

Awaiting Time

As I live and breathe, the hours
While away the passing day,
As all that quickens dies, like flowers
In springtime – beauty fades – I may
Tell the truth, and find that love
Inspires an immortality –
Night brings the dawn, the skies above,
God's realm, reach through eternity –

To succour blind humanity,
I offer gratitude, this rhyme
Might rescue hope's reality,
Even whilst awaiting time.
10th October 2017

All Triumphs

All triumphs seem to be my own –
Left to celebrate alone,
Like one whose beauty, not yet shown –

To others, lives within her art,
Reacting to strange memories,
Illusions, dreams – my very heart,
Unused to boredom, tries to please
My longing for a true perfection –
Possibly a hope beyond
Humanity – my soul's reflection
Shines – my inner joys respond.
11th October 2017

Thinking Softly (for Mother)

Thinking softly, tenderly,
Heaven knows I can't forget,
I sense you there in all I see –
Night and day, my world – and yet,
Knowing you are with me now,
Needing you, it seems, somehow,
Gratefully, I keep my vow –

Silently, to love forever,
Offering, with every breath,
Freedom for your soul, I'll never
Tire, your beauty lives through death,
Lasting through these words – and more –
Your worth, and all that's gone before.
12th October 2017

Hope Revealed

Happiness can be obscure,
Often difficult to find,
Perfect love can reassure,
Eternal truth is of the mind –

Remaining with me everywhere,
Even when I feel alone,
Virtually beyond despair,
Expressing peace within; I've grown
Accustomed to anxiety,
Like one within a world concealed,
Evolving, slowly breaking free,
Delighting in a hope revealed.
13th October 2017

Chance Words

Crystal thoughts, and angels' dreams,
Heaven's beauty, soft and still
Alive with wonder, all that seems
Naturally pure – so will
Chance words, like these, relieve your mind,
Enchant your world, and make it kind?

Whether you see loveliness,
Or only doubt, within your eyes
Remains a spark of hope – success
Defines itself, and fools are wise –
Sublime, life's mystery.
14th October 2017

Speciality

Still rearranging words, which seem
Precious to my fertile mind,
Exciting all the joy each dream
Can bring, to my delight, I find
Illusion in reality,
A fantasy within the truth,
Life a sweet uncertainty,
Inspiring me to write, as youth
Transforms the actuality,
Your world, my speciality.
15th October 2017

Easily Enough

Easily enough, I find
A world of love and fantasy
Somewhere in my heart – my mind,
Inspired, provides these words – I see
Life's beauty all around me, still
Young and lovely, so I will –

Enjoy myself, while time permits
Night and day to be my own,
Our world my prop and playground, its
Unique enchantments mine – I've grown
Gentle, through my quiet years,
Happy, as fulfilment nears.
16th October 2017

Allowing Me

Allowing me to write, I find
Life and love are much the same –
Life lingers in the mortal mind,
Or in the wind – love is its name;
Weeping tears of joy, it seems
Its inspiration comforts me,
No thoughts, desires, no heartfelt dreams
Gain precedence, as verity –

Merges life and love with truth,
Eternity with ageing youth.
17th October 2017

Letting Live

Lying in a world of dreams,
Even as my heart awakes,
Time passes slowly, and it seems
That heaven knows of man's mistakes;
Immersed in love, I close my eyes,
Night lingers, as its beauty dies,
Gently, with the dawn…

Lost within a mind that's free,
Interpreting the truth, I give
Velvet words to those who see
Enlightenment in letting live.
18th October 2017

Just Thankful

Just thankful for my world, the day
Unfolding, for my time on earth,
Silently, I feel my way
To inner paradise – it's worth –

Thinking precious thoughts, to find
Heaven ever there within,
A beauty waiting in the mind,
Never ceasing to begin
Kindling flames within the heart,
Flames of love, forever free –
Unbowed, unspent, undying art
Lives on inside its mystery.
19th October 2017

Much Missed (for Mary Brown)

Moments, minutes, hours pass
Unnoticed, as I think of you –
Could it be? But no, alas,
Heaven holds you now – the few –

Merge into the endless days
I wish that you were with us yet,
Smiling, with your loving ways –
Surely we shall not forget,
Ever – though our hearts resist
Despair, please know how much you're missed.
19th October 2017

Admittedly

Admittedly, I'm just a fool,
Dreaming through the passing years,
Marvelling, that, as a rule,
I write such poetry that nears
The depths of all my heart can feel,
Transcending life's banality –
Expressing truths, my thoughts reveal
Devotion to reality,
Like one whose very soul is free,
Yet just a fool, admittedly.
20th October 2017

Taking Time

Taking Time, I try to write
As one who loves the human mind,
Knowing very little might
Impede the process, yet I find
Near-perfect words of inspiration
Greet my efforts – contemplation –

Tells of hope – this very hour
Illuminates my thoughts – this rhyme,
Made lovely by a greater power,
Ends as it starts, by taking time.
21st October 2017

Wishing Well

Whilst writing this, it seems to me
I'm just a shadow, or a dream,
Slipping through this world, I see
Hope and happiness, yet seem
Invisible in others' eyes,
Not belonging, yet the wise
Greet the future, as it dies –

Without a qualm, into the past,
Evening falls; if time could tell,
Like fools, the truth, would beauty last,
Like love, which lives in wishing well?
22nd October 2017

Not Asking More

Never shall I cease to be
One whose soul is soaring free,
The world my own – eternity –

Attracts the words of poets, I
Speak of how it lives in dreams,
Knowing not the reason why
I sense its truth in all that seems
Near, yet somehow far away,
Gentle thoughts of yesterday –

Merging in a new tomorrow,
Offering what's gone before,
Revealing hope – I feel all sorrow
Ends in love, not asking more.
23rd October 2017

Nearly Mine

Never seeming quite alive,
Exactly as I'd wish to be,
A creature who may not survive
Reality, I've yet to see
Love's beauty shine upon my soul,
Your world reach out to me, the whole –

Multitude of life's desires –
Instinctive truths, delights divine –
None can quench eternal fires,
Enchantments which are nearly mine.
24th October 2017

Amusements

As life brings opportunities,
Moments of delight, its scope,
Unfathomed, brings its subtleties,
Sorrows and amusements; hope
Emerges from its tragedy,
Making love and truth appear,
Everyone needs comedy,
No doubt you smile at words you hear
That tickle your imagination,
So laughter feeds the hungry nation.
25th October 2017

Mistakes Made

My life is filled with many wrongs,
I'm just a sinner, blest with sorrow,
Such is the truth, which still belongs
Today, and shall remain tomorrow;
As a suppliant, I pray,
Knowing of my imperfection,
Entreating mercy; skies of grey
Shelter me, my soul's reflection –

Mirrors my unworthy mind,
And shows a debt which can't be paid,
Dawn comforts me, the love I find
Erases the mistakes I've made.
26th October 2017

Insufficiency

Insufficiency of mind
Never seems to bother me,
Somehow, I have yet to find
Uncertainty – simplicity
Flourishes within a heart
Free from any earthly care,
I feel it beat with love, my art
Creates its beauty – something there
Illuminates what little sense
Exists within what might have been
Natural intelligence –
Could my blinded eyes have seen
Your soul?
27th October 2017

Along The Thames

Along the Thames of yesterday,
Light bewildering my eyes,
On my own, I walked, the way
Nearly all have done, the wise
Grateful endlessly –

To be alive, on asking why,
Heaven sends them her reply:
Earth's waters, which reflect the sky –

Tell of love – as rivers flow,
Happily, into the sea,
As the Thames, the friend we know,
Makes his way, eternally,
Ever-changing, with the tide,
Still lovely, as I walked beside.
28th October 2017

Gemma Connor

Golden thoughts of you are mine,
Even as I start to write
My tribute, as each living line,
Made lovely by your sheer delight,
And sweet exuberance –

Creates this offering for me,
Of a beauty yours alone,
No talents, but your own, could be
Nearer to my heart – I've grown,
Out of humble admiration,
Responsive to your soul's dictation.
29th October 2017

Monday Mine

Monday mine, that day again,
Of beauty, purpose, pain and strife,
No doubt that I'm alive, and when
Dawn turns to dusk, I'll know that life
Always shall evolve, and so,
You see, my world shall breathe and grow –

Miraculously, as my mind,
Influenced by thoughts divine,
Needs only love itself, to find
Expression, on this Monday mine.
Monday 30th October 2017

To Write Again

Tomorrow turns into today,
Or so it seems, as words that play –

With soft delight, within my mind,
Rapidly, I shall forget,
I save them here, for you to find,
To cherish, or discard, and yet
Each thought was once my own –

Alive within my loveliness,
Gently glowing in my eyes,
A dream of fading truthfulness –
Imagine beauty, as it dies,
New-born, to write again.
31st October 2017

Unconcerned

Unconcerned, my solitary
Nature loves to think and dream,
Careless of reality,
Of all that we are told, I seem
Nobody in others' eyes,
Contrarily, myself, I feel
Everything – immortal, wise,
Remarkably secure – the real
Notion of success has turned
Endeavour to delight – I've learned
Discernment, yet am unconcerned.
1st November 2017

Unanswered

Unanswered questions, silent prayers,
Never heard within this earth,
Alone I listen, all my cares
Negate the truth, as time's rebirth,
Signalled by the break of day,
Waits in dreams, this very hour
Eventually slips away,
Reduced to memories, my power
Evaporates, to come again,
Dies to live – sun follows rain.
2nd November 2017

Old November

Of time, and all that's gone before,
Light fading, broken dreams, and more
Delights which end, I write – love's store –

Nears completion, old November
Offers beauty in decay,
Veiled in autumn winds; remember,
Every death brings life, and may
Move the world to loveliness,
Bring hope, as in the year's decline,
Eternal thoughts of blessedness
Renew my faith in truths divine.
3rd November 2017

Lisson Grove (for Janice)

Learning to like Lisson Grove,
I make my way there, gratefully,
Shielded from all doubts, which prove
Shades of unreality –
Once wisdom is your stated goal,
No-one can deny your soul –

Greater knowledge, so, as I
Reach for hope, a helping hand,
Offered generously, my
Very heart shall understand
Enough to fill my dreams.
4th November 2017

Naturally (for Robert Sharpe)

Naturally yours, it seems
As lovely to be with you as my
Taking time to write – my dreams
Unfold in images of why,
Right or wrong, you'll always be
A precious, true and loving friend –
Like my breath, you're there for me,
Like hope, our world need never end –
Your thoughts live on in mine.
5th November 2017

Anything Lovely (for Charles, with thanks)

Anything lovely gives me pleasure,
Nothing can take that joy away,
Yesterday was a day to treasure,
Tomorrow a thought with which to play
Happily, sadly, lovingly,
Imagining what the hours could bring,
Never was time so silently
Gentle and subtle – everything –

Leads to the new, so tell me why,
Oh why, does its truth and novelty
Vanish so quickly? You and I
Enjoy ourselves, as the world we see
Leaves us to make our way alone,
Yet never quite lost, through life's unknown.
6th November 2017

Waking Slowly

Waking slowly, gratefully
Alive within this troubled earth,
Knowledge brings uncertainty,
Imagination proves its worth,
Nightly, in our living dreams,
Gently, softly, as it seems –

Shadows of the past remain,
Like lovely, long-lost memories
Of how life used to be, again
We realize that thoughts like these
Linger through eternity –
Your day begins, mine waits for me.
7th November 2017

Offering Love

Offering love, I aim to please
Familiar and the strangest friends,
Free to see as heaven sees,
Even as her beauty lends
Reason to my arrogance,
Inspiration to the wise,
Nothing's ever left to chance,
Greatness shines from humble eyes –

Like stars within an endless night,
Or sparks of hope, their loveliness
Veering on perfection, light
Enchants the world of Godliness.
8th November 2017

Plenty Of Time

Plenty of time in which to write
Like one whose world of thoughts and dreams
Explores her very soul, which might
Never disappear – who seems
To sense life's timeless purity,
Yesterday's security –

Of mind, which lasts today, tomorrow –
Free from bitterness and sorrow –

Thankful for this perfect hour,
Inspiring this imperfect rhyme,
Marvelling at heaven's power,
Enthralling one with endless time.
9th November 2017

Before The Dawn

Before the dawn lights up the sky,
Even while the night is old,
Feeling only thankful, I
Offer up these words – I'm told
Reason waits in every mind,
Each one of us shall wake to find –

The truth, if we have eyes to see
Heaven's earthly mystery
Evolving through eternity –

Dreams that happen to be real
And tangible – when doubt is gone,
When love is all that lives, I'll feel
Night's blessing, just before the dawn.
10th November 2017

Second Best (for Mother)

Shall I ever live to be
Exactly as I was before?
Could my thoughts become as free,
Or lovely, as the truth, or more
Near perfection? In my mind,
Dreams gather, as the angels find –

Beauty almost everywhere,
Even in a heart at rest,
So your love is always there
To comfort – truth is second best.
11th November 2017

True Humanity

The world of endless love may be
Remote, a loveliness that seems
Unknown, yet mortal eyes may see
Eternity, as earthly dreams –

However strange, may still reveal
Undying shades of yesterday
Made glorious, as all we feel,
As heaven's humble children, may
Never, ever, disappear –
I sense that we may, possibly,
Together, through all doubt and fear,
Yet show our true humanity.
12th November 2017

Strange Poetry (on discovering the poetry of John Compton Miller)

Subtle, sweet word-music came
To me, as your strange poetry
Reached out to me – I found your name
As one who's blind begins to see;
No longer in the darkness, I
Gained in wisdom, light was my
Emancipation – should I die –

Perhaps, tomorrow, still I've known
Of heaven's joy within your art,
Evening falls on all who've grown
To love this earth, yet, in my heart,
Remains the beauty of your mind,
Your gift, which other eyes shall find.
13th November 2017

Timelessness

The world is slipping past my eyes
Incessantly, yet still I find
My heart beats; beauty never dies
Eternally, as, in my mind,
Love speaks of joys forever new,
Every night brings heaven's dawn,
Such is timelessness, as few
Seem to notice – when I'm gone,
Never mourn for me, I live,
Even as my thoughts survive,
Swept by winds of hope, which give
Sweet succour – endlessly alive.
14th November 2017

Life Continues

Love each hour that you behold,
In everything you say and do,
For all that lives is growing old,
Even as I write, and you –

Could live a hundred years, or might
Only last another day,
None can know what strange delight
Time might offer – still, I say,
It is enough to know the truth –
Night comes to all, and yet it ends,
Uniting us in dawn's sweet youth,
Earth breaks the hearts that heaven mends –
Sacred life continues.
15th November 2017

Proceeding

Proceeding on my chosen way,
Reacting to my hopes and dreams
Of love, the wonder of the day,
Creating poetry, which seems
Everything to me, my mind
Enlarged by earth's unfettered glory,
Delicate and strange, I find
It speaks of truth, an untold story,
None have heard, yet some may see,
Gradually, perfectly.
16th November 2017

Unaided Work

Unused to company, alone,
Needing only heaven's love,
As one remaining yet unknown,
I write of joy, as, from above,
Dawn gently greets my living eyes,
Even as its beauty dies,
Dream-like; perfect wisdom lies –

Within this strange, unaided work,
Or, should I say, this fool's conceit?
Reason shines where dangers lurk,
Kindness makes this world complete.
17th November 2017

Afterthought

As all that was may come to be,
Forever, in the human mind,
Time itself is history,
Each one of us alive to find
Reality, an afterthought,
The moment of sublime reflection,
Hope, when all this earth has taught
Only leads to dark dejection –
Unexpectedly, our hearts
Guide us to a world of light,
However blind we were, love starts
To save us from unending night.
18th November 2017

Doubtlessly

Doubtlessly, I'll write again
Of dreams and love and many things
Unusual and common – rain
Brings sunshine, dawn the dusk, which brings
The night, which always finds its end,
Light shines beyond mortality,
Entreating us to live, to send
Sweet signs of perpetuity,
Silent promises of grace,
Listen quietly, and face
Your world – you'll find a better place.
19th November 2017

Much Too Late

Much too late to think of sorrow,
Unwelcome thoughts just slip away;
Created from the past, tomorrow
Holds the beauty of today –

Together with the many things
Our little world of trouble brings,
Our souls alive – imaginings –

Lovely, in our dreaming minds,
As heaven beating in our hearts,
Tell of perfect joy, which finds
Eternal love – our journey starts.
20th November 2017

Obediently

Obediently loving, blind,
Believing life is not my own,
Enthralled by wonder, gentle, kind,
Demanding nothing – so I've grown,
In gratitude and strength, to see
Everything imagination,
New forever, seems to me,
To my delight and consternation,
Like a child, who, in her youth,
Yet feels the beauty of the truth.
21st November 2017

Easier Days

Elapsing time brings quieter hours
And gentler moments, easier days,
Subservient to heaven's powers,
I sense the evening – sun's sweet rays,
Embers in a dying fire,
Remain with me – my soul's desire –

Dreams which never seem to end,
Allusions to imagination's
Yearning for the truth, to send
Soft thoughts to soothe life's generations.
22nd November 2017

Darkly Lovely

Deep within my waking mind
Are thoughts of loveliness and night,
Reaching through the hours, I find
Knowledge of a world, which might
Leave me with the coming dawn,
Yet lingers in my heart – forlorn –

Lost, I'll never live to be,
Or tired – I'm overwhelmed with love,
Velvet images, a sea
Enveloping my soul; above,
Lies heaven's immortality,
Yesterday's eternity.
23rd November 2017

Shutting Down

Such as these ridiculously
Humdrum words inspire me now;
Unusually, particularly
Technological; somehow
They came to me, as even though
I'd seen them many times before,
Never had I come to know
Greater meaning in them – more –

Decision in their certainty
Of spirit – I can see you frown
Whilst reading this sweet poetry –
New worlds were mine, whilst 'Shutting Down'.
24th November 2017

Losing Time

Living just for love, for life,
Or every minute of the day,
Single, I remain – a wife,
In thrall, I'll never be – I may
Not seem much, yet my solitude
Gives me a broader attitude –

To everything that I perceive –
Illusive, real – within this rhyme,
My words speak truly – I believe
Exactly this: I'm losing time.
25th November 2017

Unspoilt Child

Unseen was all that lay ahead,
Never spoken was the word
'Severity', the ways that led,
Perhaps, to truth – the second, third
Or fourth instalments of my story,
Imagined in my youthful dreams,
Lie lost – forgotten hopes of glory,
Told in tales of love – it seems –

Crazy, now, to think of those
Happy, though imperfect, days,
Illusive worlds that somehow chose
Life's fantasies; as one who plays
Denied her toy – this unspoilt child.
26th November 2017

Becoming Calm

Beholding madness in my eyes,
Even as I search within,
Creating something lovely, wise,
Or sacred, helps me to begin
My journey to a better day,
I feel my way through earthly sorrow,
Near streams and fields of gladness may
God guide my thoughts, until tomorrow –

Comes, in glory, love and light,
And gentleness, as heaven's balm
Lingers in the fleeting night,
My world, my soul, becoming calm.
27th November 2017

Before We Part

Beauty is a precious thing,
Elusive love means even more,
Freedom is a song we sing
Of ecstasy, a feeling, or
Resurgent hope, a living flame,
Earth's own – a thought without a name –

Without a reason for its joy,
Enchantment, or delight – I toy –

Ponderously, with these words,
As one who's reaching for your heart,
Reaching for the wind, as birds
Touch paradise, before we part.
28th November 2017

Awaiting Words

As time ticks slowly by, I wait,
Wondering what words may come,
And, as I write, I hesitate,
Instinctively, it could be some
Truth which no-one could deny,
Illusive though it might appear,
Naturally, we live to die,
Gently passing, as the year –

Whiles away each living season,
Only to begin again,
Rain falls for a perfect reason,
Death brings life, and love is when
Such words as these survive.
29th November 2017

Additionally

As one whose object is to write
Dramatic words of joy and light,
Dauntless poetry of grace –
Imagination's child – I face
The obstacle of how to please –
If words could shine like moonlight, these
Ordinary lines would steal
Night from the heavens – you would feel,
Additionally, something new –
Love is of itself – and you,
Like seasons, changing endlessly,
Yourself, would sense what angels see.
30th November 2017

My Words Today

My words today are clear as glass –
Years of yesterdays shall pass –

Without a moment left to see
Our lives transform world history –
Reflecting on this mystery,
December dawns – its subtlety
Shows strange familiarity –

To me, a child, who feels her way,
Or walks, alone, through mists of grey,
Delighting in her thoughts, which play
A melody within, and may
Yet clarify my words today.
1st December 2017

My Ambition

My ambition is to live
Yielding just to love, to give –

And give, and never take, to write
My poetry, and not confuse
Beauty with floridity,
Illusion with reality,
Time with worlds of day or night,
Instinct with the power to choose;
Only dreaming, my condition
Never changes my ambition.
2nd December 2017

Fond Thoughts (for Robert Sharpe)

From one whose pure, devoted mind
Only thinks of you this hour
Now passing, of the world we find
Dreaming through our days – the power –

Transforming fantasy to truth,
Happy in our certainty
Of heart, the mystery of youth,
Untarnished, in our souls, as we
Gently meet and part, come these
Heartfelt words, for you alone,
To offer my fond thoughts, to please,
Say 'thank you' for the love you've shown.
3rd December 2017

Tomorrow Waits

Tomorrow waits, today begins,
Only just to disappear;
My world and yours, our virtues, sins,
Our very souls, consume each year,
Revealing beauty, ugliness,
Reason, truth, desire, delight,
Old sorrows, new-found happiness,
Within, without – as day meets night –

We live and breathe this earthly air,
As mortals, who might make their way,
Instinctively, with loving care,
To paradise – I hope we may
Survive – tomorrow waits.
4th December 2017

Fond Goodbye (for my class)

For you, I speak of how I feel,
Of why I write this fond goodbye,
Now coming from within – a real
Demonstration, proof that I –

Give thanks for you, and wish you well,
Often shall I think of you –
Our happiness – as time shall tell,
Doubtlessly, of pastures new –
Brought together, we must part,
Your worlds and mine must differ, start
Evolving – farewell, from my heart.
5th December 2017

Within My Power (for Mother)

Whilst musing on my happiness,
I think of you, as ever, then
The world is mine – its loveliness,
Heaven's own, returns again,
In memories of love, of your
Natural delight – before –

My eyes I see your sweet perfection,
Yours alone – this pure reflection –

Places you beyond all harm
Or insult, immortality
Weaves its spell, its magic charm
Enfolds you in eternity,
Remaining still within my power.
6th December 2017

My Messages

Music fills this heart of mine,
Yours to listen to, divine –

My messages of love, which seem
Eternal, as the mountain stream,
Slipping swiftly to the sea,
Softly sighing, quietly
Alive, within your very being,
Gently telling what you know,
Exactly what your eyes are seeing –
Shadows – thoughts of long ago.
7th December 2017

Sight Unseen

So shall this lovely sight unseen,
Illustrated in my mind,
Give thought to love that might have been,
Hope, a beauty of a kind
That never disappears?

Unless, within these mortal eyes,
Night's images reveal tomorrow's
Strange simplicity, which dies,
Even as it lives; my sorrows –
Every one a fading dream –
Need never trouble, it would seem.
8th December 2017

Love On My Mind

Like a wave, caressing me,
Overwhelming me, this feeling,
Very nearly heavenly,
Excites and calms my soul, revealing –

Only pure, divine emotions,
Naturally lovely – oceans –

Merging in a sea of glory,
Yesterday's, tomorrow's story –

Making music everywhere,
I sense its wonder, as I find
No-one – yet the world is there,
Delighting me, love on my mind.
9th December 2017

Fleetingly

Forming words within my mind,
Like all that's over, lost and gone,
Each illusive hour, I find,
Evolves into the coming dawn,
To fade and softly disappear,
Instinctively, I write each line,
No longer need I worry, fear
Gently vanishes; a fine,
Lustrous morning beckons me –
Youth smiles at me, so fleetingly.
10th December 2017

Popularity

Perceiving, in my solitude,
Others' pleasure, in my eyes,
Perceiving it with gratitude
Unmixed, as laughter lives and dies,
Like sunlight on an April day,
And happiness is like a dream
Realized, as clouds of grey,
Immersed in sadness, fade and seem
To welcome heaven's clarity –
Your world, my popularity.
11th December 2017

Late Rising

Late rising, when the day has started,
And my life has disappeared,
The dawn has found me muddle-hearted,
Entertaining doubts – I feared –

Reproach, yet still I seem to write,
Inspired by sloth and tardiness,
Simply seeming to delight
In indolence and laziness –
Nature's way of compromising,
Gently causing this late rising.
12th December 2017

Time Together (for Eunice)

The world is ours, this precious day,
Illuminated in my mind,
Made lovely by your joy, the way
Each moment brings so much, I find –

The minutes merge into the hours
Of gladness and delight; as I
Give thanks, our friendship blossoms, flowers
Enchantingly, it seems that my
Triumph is your own, and your
Happiness is mine, and whether
Ending or beginning, wrong or
Right, we love our time together.
13th December 2017

Silken Words

Silken words, I long to hear,
Illusions in a world that's real,
Like mysteries of love, as mere
Knowledge vanishes – I feel
Enchantment echo in my mind,
No need to fear its depths – I find –

Wonder in my soul, my heart
Only beats with passion's truth,
Remaining lovely, as we part,
Dreaming, living, ageing youth
Slips by in silken words.
14th December 2017

Secret Dreams

Secret dreams go on forever,
Early dawn brings dusk, and night
Creates its tender thoughts, which never
Reach towards a world which might
End in soft oblivion –
Time beckons, and we carry on –

Down the road to paradise,
Remaining gratefully aware
Even of the strange advice
A poet gives – does someone care,
Miraculously, as it seems
Someone knows our secret dreams?
15th December 2017

Praise Pleases

Praise pleases me, its loveliness
Releases me from earthly chains,
As kindness, with its soft caress,
Inspires these words, as heaven reigns
Supreme, I feel that I may live
Each day, if only just to give –

Part of me, my poetry,
Life's beauty running through my veins,
Embracing all humanity,
As sunshine in a sky that rains
Seemingly unendingly,
Enlightening my soul, as we
Salute the world of praise.
16th December 2017

Still Working

Still working, as my tenderness
Takes care of its divine delight,
Intricate expressiveness,
Lit by love; the ending night,
Like time itself, is gone…

Whilst my darling carriage clock,
Only small, diminutive,
Remains alive, though you may mock,
Knowing not, that as I live
I sense it in my very being,
Now felt, now heard, now almost seeing
Gentle moments pass…
17th December 2017

Your Illusion

Your illusion, sweet and clear,
Our world of loveliness and light,
Unknown, and love, forever near,
Remaining deep within us, night –

Immersed in darkness, precious day,
Living in a world that seems
Like paradise, so far away,
Unseen, except within our dreams,
Solitude and happiness,
Inspire these words – in my confusion
Or simplicity, I bless
Nature's beauty – your illusion.
18th December 2017

Ordinary Day

Overwhelmed by life, it seems
Reason brings reality;
Delighting in a world of dreams,
I sense the dawn's sweet clarity;
Night ends, I wake to morning's truth,
A universe surrounding me,
Regardless of old age or youth,
Yet lovely for my eyes to see –

Demanding nothing more, I may
Achieve but little, far away
You smile, some ordinary day.
19th December 2017

Alternatively

As I rise, I almost fall,
Like one who's feeble, weak and old,
Tired, and yet I feel that all
Eternity is mine – the cold
Reality of day begins,
Night's fantasy is of the past,
A certainty of purpose wins
The morning hours, until, at last,
I feel my work is almost done,
Very nearly over, I
Express my gratitude, as one
Living lovingly, to die
Your servant – yet, alternatively…
20th December 2017

Unfashionably

Unfashionably, as I choose
Not similarity, but beauty,
Free from slavery, I use
A word – as others pledge their duty,
Seeming always to conform;
Happy in my difference,
I seem to vary from the norm,
Or commonplace, and yet good sense,
Never mixed with arrogance,
Allows me to be understood,
Believing that I have the chance,
Like single-minded poets should
Yet have, to write unfashionably.
21st December 2017

Another For You (for Harry)

Another for you, my darling boy,
Now that Christmas time is near,
Our time together, and a toy,
To trifle with, I give – I fear
Happiness is of the mind,
Enjoyment all too brief – a kind
Realized, then left behind –

For many – yet the love we know,
Our feelings for each other, grow,
Remaining beautiful, to show –

Your constancy, and mine, is true,
Our pleasures seem forever new,
Unchanged, within these words for you.
22nd December 2017

Reclusive Love

Relying on myself, I feel
Enamoured of my solitude,
Charmed by loneliness, a real
Longing, as my attitude,
Unusual though it may seem,
Simply purifies my mind,
I write to live, and live to dream
Velvet dreams, and still I find
Everything my own…

Like one whose heart beats silently,
One whose star shines up above,
Very much alone, I'll be
Enfolded in reclusive love.
23rd December 2017

Coming Hours

Creating something lovely, I
Only think about tomorrow,
Miracles surround me, my
Instinct tells of joy, as sorrow
Never conquers love – I see
Greatness, hope's eternity –

Happy knowing strength within,
Or confidence within my heart,
Unendingly, I shall begin
Reaching through the moments, start
Surrendering the coming hours.
24th December 2017

Precious Day

Proceeding through life's every trial,
Remembering its blessings, too,
Early in the morning, while
Celebrating Christmas, through
Its beauty and its joy, I write
Of how a child was born, to bring
Undying love to us, and light,
Sublime, to shine on everything –

Dreams are real, as angels play
And sing to us, through clouds of grey –
Your hope is mine, this precious day.
25th December 2017

Hardly There

How quietly I wake and rise,
As, silently, the day begins,
Reacting slowly, as my eyes
Discover morning's darkness – sins,
Like mine, are manifold and great,
Yet heaven seems to contemplate –

The universe – whilst I, alone,
Hold my responsibility,
Every thought and deed is known,
Religion tells us – purity
Enlightens, yet is hardly there.
26th December 2017

Images In Mind

I sense them living in my heart,
Merging with my very being,
As a sinner, from the start,
God has made me mortal, seeing
Earth's delights has left me free,
Surrounded by eternity –

Instinctively, I close my eyes,
No longer shall the world despise –

My solitude and gentleness,
In nature's healing powers I'll find
Nothing but a loveliness
Depicting images in mind.
27th December 2017

INDEX

Abandoned Days	71
Additionally	102
Admittedly	82
After Resting	67
Afterthought	96
All Triumphs	77
Allowing Me	80
Along The Thames	86
Already Written	35
Alternatively	112
Always There	16
Amusements	84
Another For You	113
Another Poem	9
Antoinette	8
Anything Lovely	90
Archibald	8
As Yet Unknown	62
Autumn Rain	9
Autumn Waits	57
Awaiting Time	76
Awaiting Words	102
Awake At Last	68
Becoming Calm	101
Before I Start	25
Before Rising	45
Before The Dawn	92
Before We Part	101
Better Poetry	75
Better Things	70
Brighter Hours	33
Broken Nights	49
Chance Words	78
Childish Ways	64
Chosen Words	52
Come What Will	58
Coming Hours	114
Compliments	23
Compulsory	19
Cornucopias	32
Darkly Lovely	99
Difficulties	37
Dimmed Sight	29
Doubtlessly	97
Easier Days	98
Easily Enough	79
Easy Writing	66
Empty Hours	56
Enabling Me	43
Endeavouring	32
Enough Sleep	57
False Dreams	31
Fast Asleep	10
Feeling Happy	38
Feminine Minds	50
Finally There	13
Fleetingly	107
Fond Goodbye	105
Fond Thoughts	104
For The Moment	31
Forever Friday	35
Gemma Connor	86
Giving Poetry	52
Glad To Wake	61
Gladdened Eyes	70
Gloom Threatens	60
Graceful Days	11
Growing Old	24
Hardly There	115
Hidden From Me	27
Hidden Passions	72
Hope Revealed	78
Images In Mind	116
Immeasurably	18
Immersed In Love	74
In Awe Of You	73
Ineffectually	55
Influentially	61
Insecurity	20
Insufficiency	85

Interestingly	65		No Thoughts	51
Janice Cheatley	69		Not Asking More	83
Just Glimpsed	73		Not Without Hope	45
Just Nobody	44		Obediently	98
Just Thankful	81		Offering Love	91
Kept Living	43		Old November	89
Late Rising	108		Optimistically	53
Letting Live	80		Ordinary Day	112
Life Continues	95		Ornamentally	12
Lisson Grove	89		Out Of My Mind	37
Listening To You	71		Perhaps Tomorrow	25
Little Dreams	66		Persistently	64
Little Girl	21		Pleasing Me	40
Little Missed	54		Plenty Of Time	92
Little Violin	49		Popularity	108
Living It Up	34		Praise Pleases	110
Living Lovingly	54		Precious Day	115
Losing Time	100		Precious Time	16
Love On My Mind	107		Present Moment	50
Lovely Love	65		Pretty Words	41
Lovely Sorrow	46		Previously	46
Made For You	41		Priorities	11
Making History	76		Proceeding	95
Maternal Love	72		Promised Gift	74
Mere Poetry	28		Promised Words	15
Mistakes Made	85		Quickly Writing	62
Monday Mine	87		Quiet Wisdom	19
Month Of Mine	29		Quite Content	20
Most Important	39		Reclusive Love	114
Much Missed	81		Recommending	67
Much Too Late	97		Repeatedly	51
Much Too Tired	22		Requited Love	40
My Ambition	103		Second Best	93
My Disarray	26		Secret Dreams	110
My Messages	106		September Days	59
My Monday Waits	22		Shutting Down	99
My Patience	36		Sight Unseen	106
My Poor Child	23		Silent Thoughts	56
My Stupidity	53		Silken Words	109
My Words Today	103		Slight Regret	70
Naturally	90		Soft Silence	76
Nearly Mine	84		Soldier Boy	58

Solitary Mind	13	Unanswered	88
Speciality	79	Unconcerned	88
Still Working	111	Uneventfully	18
Strange Nights	34	Unfashionably	113
Strange Poetry	94	Unpredictably	14
Taking Time	82	Unquestioning	17
Tentatively	15	Unread Rhymes	24
Thanks To You	39	Unreadiness	27
That Time Again	60	Unrecorded	75
There You Are	63	Unspoilt Child	100
Thinking Softly	77	Unsteadily	63
Thirst For Life	21	Unwillingly	44
Three Years Old	38	Virginia Woolf	59
Time To Wonder	42	Wakeful Mind	42
Time Together	109	Waking In The Night	48
Timelessness	94	Waking Slowly	91
To Please You	30	When All Is Gone	12
To Write Again	87	Whilst Writing	14
Tomorrow Waits	104	Wishing Well	83
Too Many Words	47	With Eagerness	55
Too Much Fun	26	Within My Power	105
Transforming	33	Without My Poetry	10
Travelling	17	Wanting More	69
True Humanity	93	Your Every Day	28
Truthfully	68	Your Illusion	111
Unaided Work	96		

www.ingramcontent.com/pod-product-compliance
Lightning Source LLC
Chambersburg PA
CBHW071520040426
42444CB00008B/1738